THE ADVENTURES OF BUFFALO JOE

and the blackbird with the broken wing

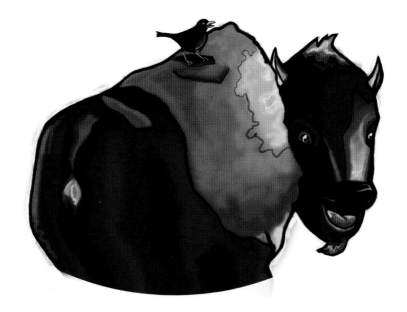

Written and Illustrated by Jamie Anne Blake

Homestead Publishing
Moose, WY • San Francisco, CA

For my Mom and Dad, who read me children's stories growing up and taught me everything important I need to know in life.

To Hal and Iola, for welcoming me into the family and introducing me to the beautiful area of Jackson Hole—truly one of the most spectacular places I know.

And for my husband Bryce, who provides constant love and support, and who gave me the idea of Buffalo Joe to begin with.

I love you!

ISBN 978-0-943972-86-2

Library of Congress Control Number 2010932975

First Edition
Printed in China

Published by
Homestead Publishing
Box 193 • Moose, WY 83012
& San Francisco, CA 94114

For other fine Homestead titles, please contact:
Mail Order Department
Homestead Publishing
Box 193 • Moose, WY 83102
or www.HomesteadPublishing.net

THE ADVENTURES OF
BUFFALO JOE

Grand Teton National Park:
A peaceful and beautiful land.
The mountains stand majestic.

The tallest peak is called The Grand.

In this place where wildflowers bloom,
and the Snake River flows,
there lives a buffalo all the animals love.

They call him **Buffalo Joe.**

Not too far down the road,
in a place called Moulton Ranch,
a blackbird's home was nestled
on a large cottonwood branch.

There, a mamma bird hatched
the eggs of her four babies.
She named the smallest one Ebony.

All the little chicks were growing big and strong,
except for little Ebony. There was something wrong.
Sure, she could chirp. Yes, she could sing.
There was only one slight problem: she was born with a broken wing.

All the other birdies fluttered their wings to fly—
except for little Ebony—which made her want to cry.
She wanted, oh so badly, to fly with all the rest,
yet her wing was smaller than the others.
She had no choice but to stay inside the nest.

One day she decided she might as well try, so she told her mother of her intentions, and chirped an excited "goodbye!"

She leapt off the nest,
soon to be air bound.

But she didn't fly at all.
In a loud *thud,*
she fell to the ground.

Every day she tried to fly,
and every day she fell.
She was bumped and bruised
and never improved
—as far as she could tell.

"Oh dear," Ebony cried,
"I'm giving up on this flying thing!
What is the use of even trying
when I have a broken wing?"

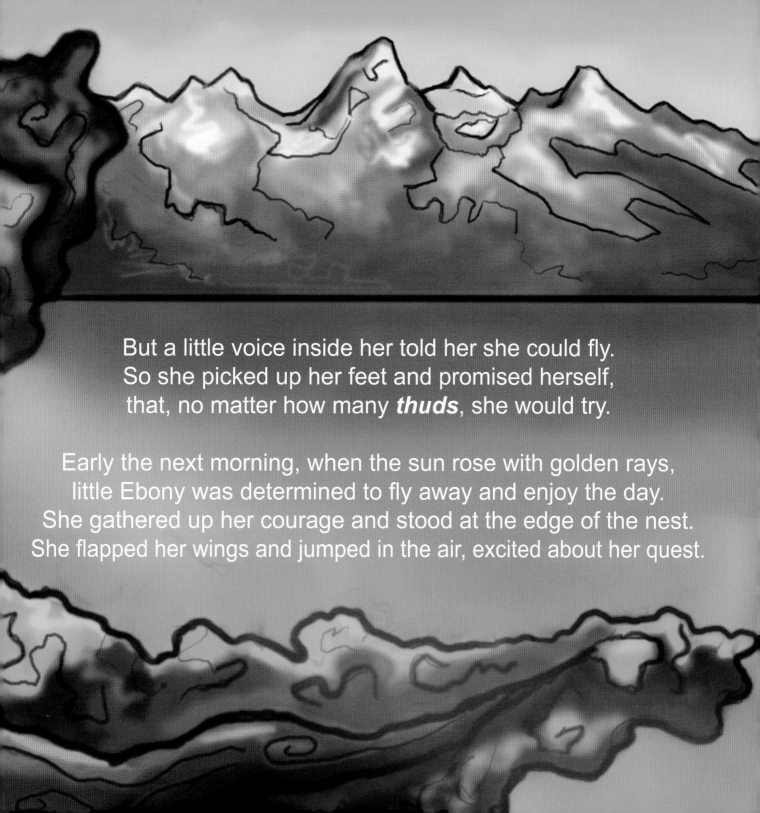

But a little voice inside her told her she could fly.
So she picked up her feet and promised herself,
that, no matter how many **thuds**, she would try.

Early the next morning, when the sun rose with golden rays,
little Ebony was determined to fly away and enjoy the day.
She gathered up her courage and stood at the edge of the nest.
She flapped her wings and jumped in the air, excited about her quest.

And fell . . .

Down,
        down below . . .

On top of a
**ROUGH,
TOUGH**
Buffalo named Joe!

Do you think Buffalo Joe
was standing there by chance?
No, my friend,
Buffalo Joe had planned this in advance.
Buffalo Joe had seen Ebony fall out of her nest every day,
and he decided he could help in this very way.

Joe felt something plop onto his back;
he turned around his head.
There stood a little blackbird
with eyes full of dread.

"No need to worry, little bird.
I'm a big buff, although
I'm friendly to all birds.
You can call me Buffalo Joe."

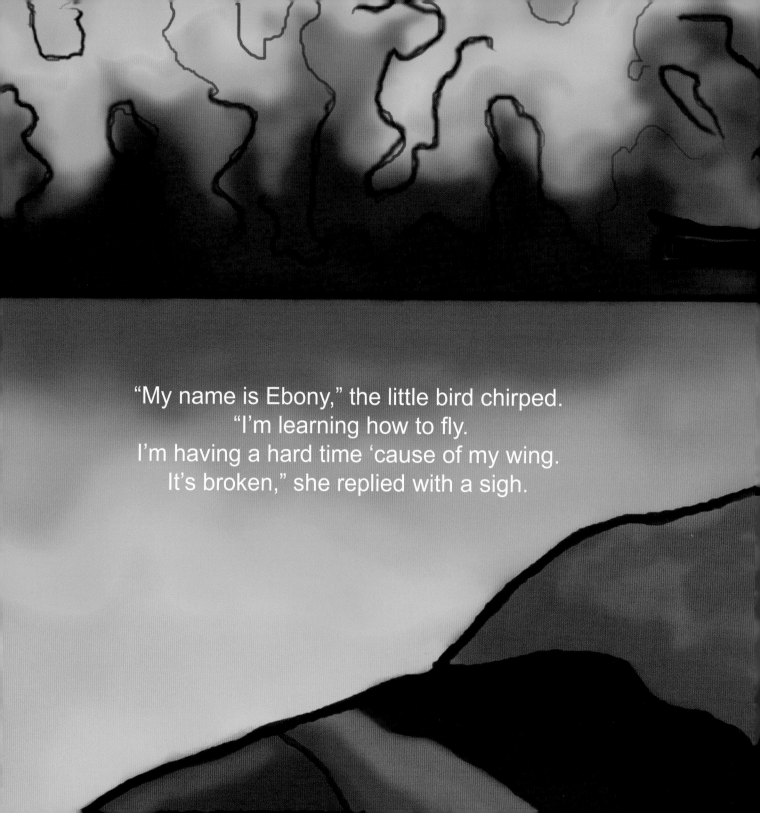

"My name is Ebony," the little bird chirped.
"I'm learning how to fly.
I'm having a hard time 'cause of my wing.
It's broken," she replied with a sigh.

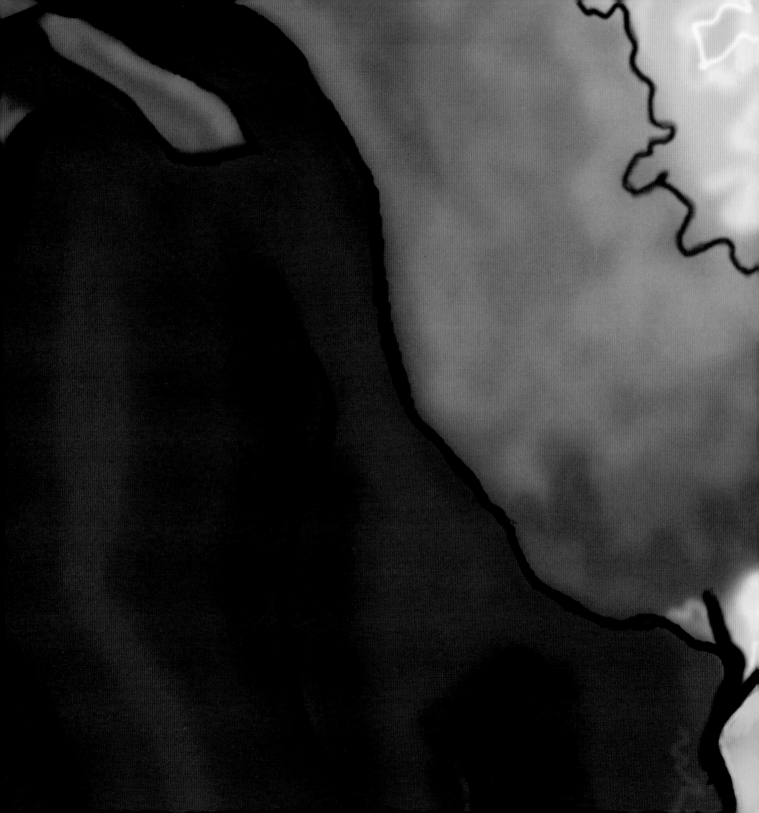

"You'll fly in no time," Joe encouraged,
"but you should give your wing a rest.
Hold on tight and we'll go for a ride.
You will be my guest!"

In a flash, off they went,
past Antelope Flats and Blacktail Butte.
Through meadows and fields they wandered,
on no particular route.

They explored Signal Mountain,
Mount Moran and Jackson Lake.
When it was time to go home,
Joe just followed the Snake.

And so the two became the best of friends—
Buffalo Joe and Ebony.
Often Ebony perched on Joe's back
and they roamed, wild and free.
Every day Ebony would try to fly—
but instead of falling to the ground . . .

she would fall on Joe's furry back,
landing safe and sound.

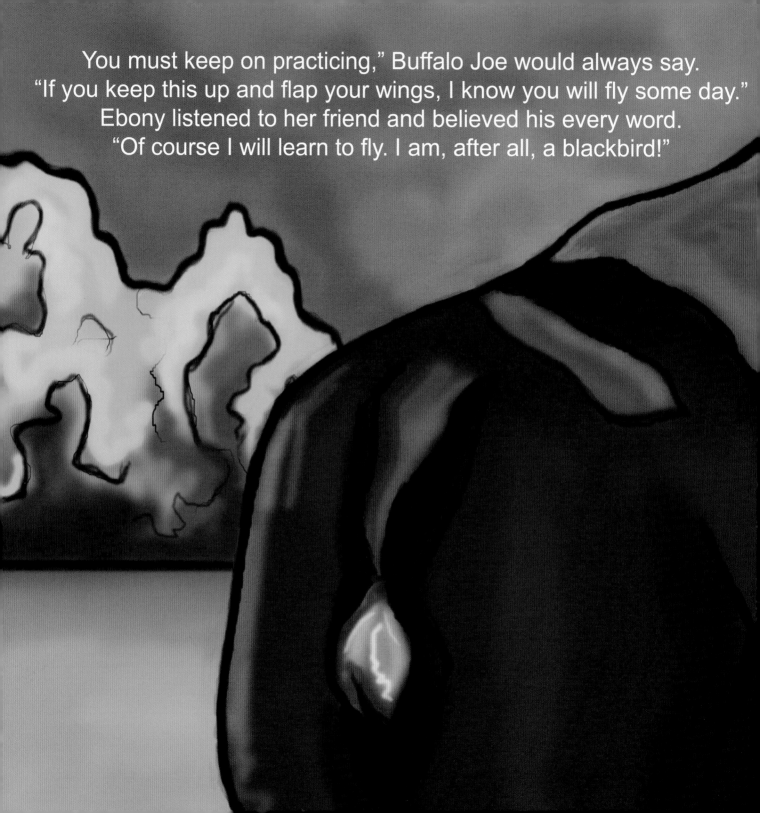

You must keep on practicing," Buffalo Joe would always say.
"If you keep this up and flap your wings, I know you will fly some day."
Ebony listened to her friend and believed his every word.
"Of course I will learn to fly. I am, after all, a blackbird!"

After a long morning of relaxation
on Buffalo Joe's back,
Ebony decided to look for worms—
she needed a tasty snack.
She hopped down and headed to the ranch
where there was wet, green grass.
Little did she know a cat named Mo
was watching her very path.

Mo crouched in the shadows,
ready to pounce on his prey.

Buffalo Joe saw the danger
and bolted towards them,
without delay.

All of this commotion
gave Ebony quite a fright.
So she spread her wings,
jumped up in the air . . .

And took off
in flight!

High up in the air, Ebony looked down to see Buffalo Joe.
He grunted and jumped, then shouted, "Hey, way to go!"
Ebony flew high in the sky and felt the wind in her wings—
Through the woods, meadows, and fields—
above the mountains and streams.

Soon it was dark and Ebony slowed down to go home,
back to the place where her best friend, the buffalo, roamed.
Buffalo Joe was waiting anxiously when Ebony arrived.
"I couldn't have done it without you," the little bird cried.

Ebony and Joe remained the best of friends
as the days and seasons went by.
It didn't make any difference that Ebony knew how to fly.
What a perfect pair—a buffalo with brown fur,
and a bird with feathers so black.
And to this day you can see the blackbird
riding on Buffalo Joe's back.

The End

About the Author/Illustrator

Jamie Anne Blake was born and raised in Northern Utah. She is the youngest of three girls, and her parents are both teachers.

One of her favorite things growing up was reading. She loved looking at the colorful illustrations, and how the pictures brought the story to life--one of the reasons why she chose the career path of writing and illustrating children's books.

After high school, she moved to Rexburg, Idaho where she attended Brigham Young University-Idaho and recieved a Bachelors of Science in Art in 2009.

There at school, Jamie met her husband, Bryce. They now live in Virginia, where they are starting their next adventure.

Photo by Erin Langford